Green Technology

Solar, Wind, and Other Alternatives

Table of Contents

Chapter 1. Introduction

From the shifting sands of immense deserts harnessing the concentrated power of the sun, to the high-altitude wind turbines capturing the invisible gusts of wind, the world is increasingly turning to green technologies as a path towards sustainable energy. Our special report uncovers the revolutionary strides in technologies such as solar, wind, and other renewable energy sources that are transforming the energy sector. Yet, while the science might seem intricate, we're determined to bring it down to earth for you. This enlightening report demystifies complex concepts, offering a clear and comprehensible insight into how alternative energy sources hold the key to a cleaner, greener future. Come with us on this journey of discovery; together, we'll explore the awe-inspiring inventiveness of engineers around the world and the potential that green technology holds for revolutionizing our energy system.

Chapter 2. The Power of the Sun: Understanding Solar Energy

Solar energy, amongst the many forms of renewable energy sources we have discovered, retains an impressive potential due to its vast availability and non-depletive nature. By tapping into this robust and continuous energy supply, we can address the pressing need for sustainable energy solutions, lessen our dependency on finite resources, and combat global climate change.

2.1. Harnessing Solar Rays

The primary technology for harnessing solar energy lies in photovoltaic (PV) cells, commonly known as solar panels. PV cells operate by absorbing sunlight, which excites the electrons in the atom of the PV cell's semiconductor material, typically silicon. The excited electrons then move across an electrical circuit, generating electricity.

A network of PV cells aggregates to form a solar panel, with multiple panels installed together as a solar array. The larger the array, the greater the electricity generation. But the efficacy of energy generation is also influenced by factors such as location, angle of installation, weather conditions, and the efficient conversion of the received solar energy.

2.2. Solar Energy Conversion Process

A PV device's sunlight-to-electricity conversion process is

fascinatingly complex and precise. To initiate the conversion, photons, or particles of light, knock electrons free from atoms, a process known as the photoelectric effect, generating a flow of electricity.

When sunlight strikes the PV cell, some photons get absorbed into the uppermost layer of the cell's silicon structure, which is doped with phosphorous to have spare electrons. The energy offered by photons is absorbed by these excess electrons, elevating their energy state and enabling them to leap into the conduction band, where they become free electrons. These free electrons are enticed across an electric field (present within the solar cell) towards the silicon layer doped with boron that lacks electrons. The flow initiated by these moving electrons is what we call electricity.

As simple as this might seem, a large part of the absorbed sunlight becomes waste heat instead of electric current. Thus, scientists are consistently probing methods to improve the efficiency of this conversion, with high-end solar panels reaching around 20%.

2.3. Silicon's Role in Solar Technology

Silicon is the fundamental ingredient for most solar technology because of its semi-conductive properties. Silicon structures form a crystal lattice that allows electrons to move and generate electric currents when excited.

Each silicon atom consists of 14 electrons, arranged in three energy bands. The useful electrons for electricity generation in silicon lie in the outer band, also known as the valence band, which holds four electrons. When energy is introduced, ideally in the form of sunlight, these electrons can get excited to the conduction band, where they are move freely and generate electricity.

Silicon's abundant availability in the earth's crust and its helpful properties make it the preferred substance for solar panel manufacturing, although researchers are exploring other materials, like perovskites, for higher efficiency and flexibility.

2.4. Solar to Storage

With the intermittent nature of solar energy—dependent on the day-night cycle and weather conditions—energy storage becomes a crucial factor for maintaining a continuous supply. Solar energy may be stored using battery systems or thermal energy storage where solar heat is saved to generate electricity in non-sunny periods.

Battery systems are broadly classified into two types: lithium-ion batteries and vanadium redox flow batteries. Lithium-ion batteries are highly efficient but have a short lifespan and are prone to safety hazards. Flow batteries, on the other hand, offer greater safety and expanded lifespan but at a higher cost and lower round-trip efficiency.

2.5. Concentrated Solar Power (CSP)

Along with photovoltaics, Concentrated Solar Power (CSP) plays a vital role in extracting energy from the sun. CSP uses lenses or mirrors to focus a large area of sunlight into a small beam. The concentrated light is then used as a heat source for a conventional power plant.

A significant advantage of CSP over PV technology is the ability to store energy for use when the sun is not shining, thereby overcoming the significant limitation of solar. Furthermore, CSP plants produce electricity on a large scale, making them viable options for powering cities and industries.

2.6. The Environmental Impact and Sustainable Development

Solar energy, being a clean and renewable source of energy, has a markedly low environmental impact compared to conventional energy sources. It does not emit greenhouse gases during operation, reduces dependence on fossil fuels, and uses significantly less water.

But, like any technology, the manufacturing and disposal of solar technology do have environmental implications. Manufacturing PV cells requires mining and purifying silicon, which can have detrimental environmental impacts if not managed properly. Therefore, the focus is currently on creating sustainable, efficient processes for the manufacturing and end-of-life handling of PV cells.

With advancements in technology and increased efficiency, solar energy has the potential to be a substantial part of our transition towards a sustainable future. As the science further refines and the green economy extends, the harnessing of the sun's immense power could bring revolutionary changes to our energy system and way of life.

Chapter 3. Harnessing the Wind: The Mechanics of Wind Turbines

Harnessing the fertile momentum of the wind is one of the oldest forms of energy capture known to humanity, and today, wind turbines stand as a testament to just how far we've come. Still, these towering structures, cropping up on landscapes across the world, often elicit wonder and curiosity. Just how do they work? What is the complex science behind their spinning blades? In this enlightening discussion, we dive deep into the mechanics of wind turbines.

3.1. The Anatomy of a Wind Turbine

Let's start with a basic breakdown of the wind turbine's structure. In essence, a wind turbine consists of three primary parts, the blades (or rotor), the nacelle (containing the gearbox and generator), and the tower.

Why do wind turbines generally have three blades? Even though one blade would be simpler and cheaper to manufacture, it would be less efficient and produce significant vibration. Adding an additional blade significantly increases efficiency and reduces vibration. However, the leap from three to four blades doesn't yield significant improvements in efficiency, yet it increases production costs. Thus, the three-bladed turbine has become a standard.

Inside the nacelle, a key component is the gearbox that steps up the rotor's slow speed to run the high-speed generator, which typically produces electricity at around 50-60Hz.

The turbine's tower is a significant part; it isn't just there for height. The tower's interior provides access for maintenance, houses the power cables, and also provides additional structural support.

3.2. The Wind and the Blade: A Dance of Energy

Wind energy is first and foremost kinetic energy. When the wind strikes the turbine blades, the aerodynamic design lifts and rotates the blades, converting some of the wind's kinetic energy into mechanical energy. The efficiency of this energy conversion process is summarized by the Betz' Law, which states that no turbine can capture more than 59.3% of the kinetic energy in wind.

Why not 100%, you might wonder? The rest of the wind's energy is needed to carry away the deflected wind to allow more wind to approach the turbine. If 100% of the wind's kinetic energy were harnessed, the wind would stop, and no additional energy could be harvested.

3.3. Ascent to Power: The Internal Mechanics

The gearbox, principally located within the nacelle atop the tower, is the cornerstone of converting raw, spinning mechanical energy into electricity that can be utilized. The primary shaft connects to the turbine blades and turns with them, typically at 10-20 rotations per minute (rpm). The gearbox is then used to step up these revolutions to the required speed for the generator, typically around 1500-2000 rpm.

When the gearbox spins at the necessary speed, it spins a magnet within the generator. In turn, the spinning magnet creates a flow of electrons - electricity. The power is then transferred via power cables running down the inside of the tower to a transformer that adjusts the voltage level for transmission over the power grid.

3.4. Turbulence and Towers: Reaching for the Sky

The height of the turbine is another critical factor in its efficiency. Wind speed increases with distance from the ground, due to less friction the higher one goes. Therefore, the taller the tower, the higher the average wind speed the turbine can harness.

3.5. The Future of Wind Technology: Bigger, Stronger, More Efficient

Technological advancements ensure wind turbines are becoming larger, significantly increasing their power output. The design of the individual components is also being continuously refined – especially the nacelle with its gearbox and generator, the blades, and lastly the materials of the turbines themselves. Blades that flex to adjust to wind speeds and directions, gearless turbines, and offshore wind farms are all pieces of this growing puzzle towards more efficient wind energy harnessing technology.

To sum it up, harnessing the wind might sound like a simple task of placing a turbine on a windy hill, but the mechanics behind are indeed intricate and fascinating. Yet, unraveling these complexities shows us just how far we've come and the promise that these green technologies bring to an energy-hungry world.

Chapter 4. Renewable Reign: Why Green Technology Matters

Renewable energy, or green technology, is becoming a pivotal player in our energy landscape. As the world grapples with the dire implications of a changing climate, it has become imperative to transition from fossil fuels, which are largely responsible for global greenhouse gas emissions, to sources that are renewable and emit minimal carbon: solar, wind, hydropower, bioenergy, and geothermal power. Economical, sustainable, and able to meet the world's rising energy demands, these renewable power sources are emerging as critical catalysts for a healthier planet and more resilient societies.

4.1. The Need for Green Technology

Climate change is no longer an abstract dystopian concept meant for future generations to grapple with. It's happening here and now, bearing grim realities and severe consequences. Unprecedented global warming is leading to the melting of polar ice caps, increasing levels of sea and intensifying extreme weather events. Meanwhile, air pollution resultant from burning fossil fuels is causing horrendous health issues, with WHO reporting that around seven million people die annually due to exposure to fine particles in polluted air. While these scenarios paint a gloomy and dark image of the future, there is a ray of hope: renewable energy.

Renewable energy technologies have the power to not only mitigate climate change by reducing carbon emissions but also enhance public health, create jobs, and bolster economies. Unlike coal or oil, which exist in finite quantities and extract a heavy environmental toll, renewable energy is plentiful and comes with minimal ecological impact.

4.2. The Solar Wave

Solar energy, hailing from the eternal furnace of the Sun, is one of the most promising sources of renewable energy. It's abundant, accessible worldwide, and emits zero pollution when it's generated. Photovoltaic (PV) cells, often assembled into solar panels, are deployed to capture sunlight and transform it directly into electricity. As the price of these technologies continues to plummet, they've become a competitive source of energy even against fossil fuels in many regions of the world.

Solar installations vary from small rooftop systems for households, to utility-scale solar farms spanning acres of land. These different solar systems synergistically work to reduce the reliance on the conventional power grid, hence minimizing carbon emissions.

Yet, for all its advantages, solar power is not without its challenges. The main issue is its intermittent nature: no power is generated at night and output can vary during the day. This necessitates the need for efficient energy storage systems or fostering a strong energy mix to offset these deficits.

4.3. Wind Power Unleashed

Like solar, wind power is seeing an annual increase in capacity, contributing significantly towards renewable energy consumption. The principles behind a wind turbine are simple yet incredibly effective - wind turns the blades, which spin a shaft connected to a generator, producing electricity.

Wind farms can be installed onshore or offshore. While the former is generally more prevalent due to lower installation costs, the latter has the potential to generate more electricity due to much stronger and reliable winds. In fact, Europe is spearheading this development, given its accessible seas and ambitious carbon-neutral targets.

Again, like solar, wind power does suffer from intermittency issues. However, advancing technology and smart grid systems help to alleviate these challenges.

4.4. The Power of Water, Bioenergy and Earth's Heat

Hydropower, arguably the oldest form of renewable energy, harnesses the huge kinetic energy of water to generate power. It's a reliable source of electricity, providing a base load of power and offering excellent storage capabilities to balance the grid.

Bioenergy, derived from organic material like plant and animal waste, is another renewable energy source worth noting. The generation process involves the burning of biomass or converting it into other forms like methane gas or transportation fuels such as bio-diesel.

Then there's geothermal power, leveraging the limitless heat stored beneath Earth's surface. By pumping water underground into hot rock formations and then back to the surface, it's possible to generate steam which drives a turbine connected to an electricity generator.

4.5. Investment in Technologies and Infrastructure

The success of a renewable energy future heavily relies on investment in technologies and infrastructure. Strategies involving smart grid technologies, demand response, advanced forecasting for renewable energy production and more effective energy storage systems are all key.

4.6. Conclusion

Green technology is on the cusp of significantly transforming the world's energy systems for the better. The transition is not only an environmental necessity but could also instigate an era of global prosperity. Each country's renewable energy path will be different, shaped by its resources and specific needs, promising a future where energy security and sustainability stand at its core.

Chapter 5. Dark Horses of Renewable Energy: Geothermal and Tidal Power

In the vast array of renewable energy options, solar and wind energy often take the spotlight. Still, two lesser-known sources hold enormous potential for unlocking a sustainable future, waiting patiently just beneath the surface of our international discussions: geothermal and tidal power. Unwavering and unwearied by the fickle moods of the weather, these power sources derive their strength from the Earth itself.

5.1. Unearthing the Potential of Geothermal Energy

Geothermal energy harnesses the Earth's inner warmth—capturing heat stored beneath our feet and converting it into a sustainable power source. This process dates back to ancient civilizations, utilizing the planet's natural hot springs for heating.

With modern technology, we can now devise ingenious applications using this naturally occurring energy. Approaching this resource, one finds that typical geothermal power plants work in three principal ways—dry steam, flash steam, and binary cycle.

The dry steam method, the most straightforward of the three, channels steam from beneath the Earth's surface to power a turbine connected to an electric generator. The flash steam method, which is the most commonly used, passes hot water at high pressures through a system where it "flashes" or rapidly transforms into steam; this steam then powers a turbine. Lastly, binary cycle plants pass hot water through a heat exchanger, which transfers the heat to a different fluid (a binary fluid)—typically an organic compound with a low boiling point—that vaporizes and drives a turbine.

Geothermal energy possesses a significant advantage over many other renewable energy types—consistency. Unlike solar or wind power, geothermal is not dependent on the weather, thereby offering a constant, reliable energy source.

However, the challenge lies in identifying suitable locations. Geothermal energy largely depends on tectonic activity. Regions situated along the Pacific Ring of Fire, for example, offer prime locations for harvesting geothermal power. Of course, technological advancements, such as enhanced geothermal systems (EGS), can artificially generate geothermal plants in areas devoid of naturally occurring geothermal resources.

=== Unleashing the Power of the Tides

The moon and Earth share a gravitationally-bound dance that generates ocean tides—massive movements of seawater capable of releasing tremendous energy amounts. This is the premise behind harnessing tidal energy—a remarkably abundant, predictable, and green source of power.

Tidal power stations operate in two crucial forms—tidal range and tidal stream systems. Tidal range systems, or "barrages," use a barrage (or dam) across an estuary. The incoming tides fill up the estuary, and upon ebbing, water is released through turbines, producing electricity.

Tidal stream systems, a newer technology, are similar to underwater windmills. They place turbines in fast-flowing tidal waters, where the moving water spins the turbine, producing electricity. These systems are less invasive than barrages and have less environmental impact, though they are currently less efficient.

Tidal power has significant promise, given its predictability. Unlike solar or wind, tides are highly consistent, following the moon's gravitational pull. Moreover, given that over 70% of the Earth's surface is water, the potential for tidal power seems nearly limitless.

However, tidal power also faces its set of challenges. Installing tidal infrastructure can be expensive and complicated by harsh marine environments. Moreover, humanity's understanding of the long-term impacts on marine ecosystems remains limited.

Overall, both geothermal and tidal power present significant potential for green energy solutions. Despite the challenges faced by these dark horses of renewable energy, their potential in contributing towards a cleaner, greener future is undeniable. Recognizing and overcoming these barriers necessitates stringent research, policy support, and public awareness. With these conditions met, we can dive deeper into Earth's vast resources and harvest the immense force for a sustainable future. As we continue to explore these alternative energy sources, so too do we find ourselves connecting not only with our modern technology but also with ancient forces, dating back millennia. It's this blend of past and future, of land and sea, that makes the exploration of these dark horses a ride worth taking. And in so doing, bring us yet another step closer to a sustainable future.

Chapter 6. Biomass Energy: From Waste to Power

Biomass energy, also known as bioenergy, is produced from organic material - the biomass - originating from plant or animal sources. Primary sources of biomass include agricultural crops, waste wood from logging and wood manufacturing, and solid waste. It's a renewable source of energy akin to wind, solar, and geothermal energy, available to us in vast quantities if harvested and utilized efficiently.

6.1. The Science Behind Biomass Energy

Unbeknownst to many, biomass energy results from a simple process that involves converting organic materials into energy-rich compounds. This process begins with photosynthesis - nature's primary mechanism for converting sunlight into chemical energy stored within plant cells.

Plants naturally absorb sunlight and carbon dioxide (CO_2) from the Earth's atmosphere. Through photosynthesis, these reactants are synthesized into sugars, which supply the plant with essential energy. When these plant materials die or are consumed by animals, the stored energy gets transferred and remains conserved within the biomass.

Burning biomass or processing it through other thermal, chemical, or biochemical methods releases this stored energy. The energy harnessed can then power various systems, such as steam turbines that generate electricity or industrial processes that require heat.

6.2. Sources of Biomass

Understanding the sources of biomass and their respective potential for energy is an essential aspect of this green technology. The following are some of the main sources of biomass used for energy production:

- Agricultural crops and waste materials: These commonly include energy-dense crops, such as switchgrass or miscanthus, as well as residues like corn stalks and wheat straw. These residues are a byproduct of food production processes and offer a source of energy that does not compete with food needs.

- Wood and Wood Processing Wastes: Waste from lumber and woodworking processes – such as sawdust, bark, and other residuals – are a substantial source of biomass. Even fallen limbs, treetops, and non-commercial species from logging operations are used.

- Animal manure and human sewage: Both of these waste streams can be anaerobically digested to produce biogas, a mixture of methane and carbon dioxide, and used as a renewable energy source.

6.3. Conversion Methods: From Biomass to Energy

Broadly, there are three biomass-to-energy conversion methods: thermochemical (pyrolysis and gasification), biochemical (anaerobic digestion), and chemical (esterification).

The thermochemical conversion process involves heating biomass in the absence (pyrolysis) or limited presence (gasification) of oxygen. Pyrolysis produces a liquid bio-oil, whereas gasification yields syngas - a mixture of hydrogen and carbon monoxide.

Biochemical conversion uses bacteria or other microbes to digest the biomass in an oxygen-free environment, in a process known as anaerobic digestion. It primarily produces methane and carbon dioxide, known collectively as biogas.

Lastly, the chemical conversion method, such as esterification, transforms vegetable oils, animal fats, or other lipids into biodiesel, a biofuel suitable for use in diesel engines, with properties similar to petroleum diesel.

6.4. The Current Landscape of Biomass Energy

Despite a long history threaded throughout every civilization as an energy source - from firewood in traditional hearths to charcoal in conventional steel production - biomass as an energy source is underutilized on a global scale. Nevertheless, there is an increasing trend among nations to tap into this resource.

The rise of biomass energy projects worldwide represents a paradigm shift from traditionally mining non-renewable fossil fuels to growing renewable biomass. The circumvention of long geological processes to obtain fuels allows for near-zero net carbon emissions, promising a greener way to satiate our energy needs.

6.5. The Future of Biomass Energy

In spite of the promise it holds, the biomass energy industry, like any nascent field, faces headwinds. Its low energy density and generally dispersed nature make it a challenge to collect and process efficiently. There are also concerns over competition for land resources that could be used for food production or conserved for ecological benefits.

Nonetheless, as technology advances, so too does the potential to overcome these obstacles. Promising research in areas like advanced biofuels, algae-based bioenergy, and genetic improvements of energy crop yield could revolutionize the field of biomass energy.

Through its unique ability to use waste materials productively, biomass energy presents an opportunity to tackle not just our energy challenges, but also waste management and rural agricultural development challenges. With continued technological evolution and strategic implementation, it could play a substantial role in the global shift towards sustainable energy.

Chapter 7. Hydropower: The Ancient Energy Source Forging Our Future

Hydropower, quite understandably, is often viewed as an old, perhaps antiquated form of renewable power given that its principles have been harnessed for many centuries. Yet, in its modern form, with consistent technological enhancements, this energy source is being reimagined and is once again at the forefront of the sustainable energy revolution.

7.1. The Principles of Hydropower

Hydropower is predicated on the fundamental principle of turning potential energy from flowing or still water into usable electricity. What might appear simple in an elementary explanation becomes quite vast when we dive into the specifics of a functioning hydropower plant.

The vibrant ecosystem of a hydropower plant is built around a reservoir that holds a massive quantity of water, typically behind a large wall known as a dam. When required, the gates of the dam are opened, releasing the water at high pressure through connected passages to an electricity generation device known as a turbine. As the water runs through the turbine, it spins the turbine blades, which in turn, are connected to an electricity generator.

This generator uses sophisticated principles of electrical engineering, where, through a synchronous generator, the mechanical energy is converted into electrical energy through the phenomenon of electromagnetic induction. The dam, though it seems like a passive entity in this framework, plays a crucial role in regulating and maintaining this ecosystem's equilibrium.

The water's release is carefully controlled to ensure a consistent supply of energy and keep the ecosystem in balance. These waters then flow away, often to rejoin the river from which they were initially collected, thus maintaining a circular water cycle within the hydropower plant.

7.2. Harnessing Hydropower: A Journey Through Time

Understanding the journey of hydropower through history helps shed light on how it's paced over centuries from being an integral part of ancient civilizations to powering the modern world. Equivalently, it has witnessed peaks and troughs in usage, both driven by the human requirement and technological evolution.

The earliest documented usage of hydropower dates back to the ancient Greeks, who used water wheels for milling. It was not until the 19th century, however, that the technology's true potential began to be recognised as a viable power source.

The evolution of hydropower over the centuries demonstrates the compelling role technology plays in energy transition while revealing our historical interdependence with this water-driven energy. As the technology evolved during the industrial revolution, hydropower entered a golden age in the late 19th and early 20th centuries with the advent of electricity generation.

7.3. Contemporary Hydropower Technologies

Contemporary hydropower plants are not just about harnessing the potential energy of waterfalling water. The different forms that this technology takes are a testament to human ingenuity. The three primary contemporary forms have their own unique characteristics and strengths, each offering a different way to harness the latent energy in water.

The first is 'Run-of-the-river' systems. This format is often used in more modest-sized rivers and streams, foregoing the presence of a reservoir. The flow of the river is used to turn the turbines, producing a remarkably consistent source of power without the ecological concerns associated with large dams.

The second are 'Storage' or 'Reservoir' systems, where a large dam maintains a reservoir of water. This configuration allows control over the water flow and quantity released to the turbines, making this type more flexible and potent than run-of-the-river designs.

Significantly, there is also the 'Pumped storage' system. This method refers to a specific context where power demand is inconsistent. At a time of low demand (and often lower power cost), water is actively pumped into a higher reservoir using excess electricity. This stored water is then released to generate power during peak demand periods, essentially acting as a large-scale battery.

7.4. Future Challenges and Prospects of Hydropower

With climate change becoming an ever-critical concern, hydropower stands front and centre as a key part of our sustainable future. It provides a range of environmental advantages, such as low greenhouse gas emissions, and energy security benefits. However, the path forward also presents certain challenges.

One significant challenge is the potential adverse ecological effect of large dams, ranging from local flora and fauna disturbances, changes in water temperature, to broader impacts on river systems. But technological advancements are expected to ease some of these issues, with promising developments in areas such as fish-friendly turbines and improved dam designs.

Additionally, hydropower's compatibility with other renewable energy sources poses fantastic potential. By combining hydropower with other green energy sources, we might be able to maximise each technology's strengths, striking a balance between reliability and sustainability, while driving towards our clean energy future. This potential could escalate hydropower's importance in the realm of renewable energy.

It's evident that the future of hydropower relies on striking a fine balance between environmental considerations and the growing energy demand. But with its historical resilience and continuous technological advancements, hydropower rightfully seems set to continue its role as an integral part of our global sustainable energy solution.

In conclusion, hydropower might be an ancient concept, but its future seems as bubbling as a river in springtime, symbolising a surge in sustainable energy that will help to forge our future. The opportunity is immense. The potential is awe-inspiring. The time for hydropower to reinvent itself for a greener future is now.

Chapter 8. Curbing Our Carbon Footprint: The Environmental Impact of Switching to Renewable Energy

Renewable energy sources are paramount not simply because they are inexhaustible, but also because they have a less harmful impact on the environment compared to conventional energy sources. This reduction in harm comes chiefly from fewer carbon emissions, which decrease the overall carbon footprint.

8.1. The Issue With Carbon Emissions

Carbon emissions — or the releasing of greenhouse gases (GHGs) into the atmosphere — is frequently tied to conventional energy systems that use fossil fuels. These fuels, when burned, produce carbon dioxide (CO_2), a potent greenhouse gas that contributes to global warming and climate change. The Intergovernmental Panel on Climate Change (IPCC) reports that electricity and heat production account for more than 25% of global GHG emissions.

Adding to the carbon burden, extraction and transportation of fossil fuels also release significant quantities of methane, another potent greenhouse gas. The reclamation process of land after mining, often done inadequately, leaves areas deforested or barren, reducing the global capability for natural carbon sequestration.

These far-reaching consequences of fossil fuel use contrast starkly with renewable energy sources that depend on naturally replenished resources, such as sunlight, wind, water, and geothermal heat.

8.2. Lower Carbon Emissions With Renewable Energy

Switching to renewable energy offers a major solution to reduce carbon emissions drastically. Solar power, for instance, generates electricity without CO_2 or other air pollutants. According to the U.S. Environmental Protection Agency (EPA), a typical residential solar panel system will eliminate three to four tons of carbon emissions each year—the equivalent of planting over 100 trees annually.

Similarly, wind energy is a pollution-free, infinitely sustainable form of energy. It doesn't emit air pollutants or greenhouse gases, according to the U.S. Department of Energy. Other sources, like hydroelectric and geothermal energy, contribute far less CO_2 compared to fossil fuels.

Even bioenergy, which does release CO_2 when burned, is considered carbon-neutral because the plants grown for biomass capture a nearly equal amount of CO_2, maintaining a balanced carbon cycle.

8.3. Coal-to-Clean Transitions

Coal-fired power plants are the biggest carbon polluters, with a single plant generating millions of tons of CO_2 annually. The swift replacement of coal with renewable energy systems is a key part of decreasing carbon emissions on a global scale.

This transition, currently happening in various parts of the world, shows promising reductions in carbon emissions. The Sierra Club's Beyond Coal campaign estimates that the coal-to-clean energy transition has reduced U.S. emissions by 10% from 2010 to 2019.

These transitions also provide opportunities for job creation in the renewable sector, mitigating job losses in the fossil fuel industry.

8.4. Energy Efficiency and Conservation

Reducing our carbon footprint isn't just about the switch to renewable energy; it's also about using energy more efficiently. Minimizing energy waste reduces the demand for energy, and as such, the carbon emissions from energy production.

Energy conservation techniques, like using energy-efficient appliances, improving insulation in buildings, or simply turning off unused lights, can reduce the individual's carbon footprint significantly. In combination with a switch to green energy systems, these measures provide a comprehensive approach to reducing carbon emissions globally.

8.5. Decentralization of Power Grids

Decentralized renewable energy production is another effective means for curbing carbon emissions. Large, centralized power plants lose a substantial portion of energy during transmission, up to 6% according to the World Bank. With decentralized renewables like solar panels or small wind turbines, energy is produced close to where it's used, vastly minimizing transmission losses.

Decentralized systems also have lower infrastructure and maintenance costs, adding to their environmental and economic benefits.

8.6. Future Perspectives

The potential for the reduction of carbon emissions through

renewable energy and energy-efficient practices is immense, but addressing this isn't without challenges. Large-scale infrastructure change, policy support, social acceptance, and considerable initial investments are needed.

However, with increasing recognition of the urgent need to decrease carbon emissions, alongside falling costs and technological advancements in renewables, the future of sustainable, low-carbon energy systems is not just possible—it's increasingly probable.

The world is shifting towards a green energy revolution. Every solar panel installed, every wind turbine erected, every energy-saving measure taken, and every policy in support of renewable energy represents a step towards a more sustainable, lower carbon future. By choosing renewable options and making efficient use of our energy, we're curbing our carbon emissions and combating climate change—one kilowatt-hour at a time.

Chapter 9. Economic Implications: Cost and Returns of Renewable Energy Investments

Economic considerations are a key determinant in the shift towards renewable energy, with the benefits expanding well beyond purely environmental objectives. In this section, we'll explore the costs associated with investing in renewable energy and the potential returns these investments can yield, delving into factors like payback periods, government incentives, market conditions, and socio-economic implications.

9.1. Initial Investment and Operating Costs

The monetary commitment required to transition to renewable energy consists of two main components: the initial investment and ongoing operational costs. The initial investment, or capital cost, covers the purchase and installation of the technology. Operational costs include routine maintenance, repairs, and, in some cases like bioenergy, fuel costs.

The initial investment for renewable energy systems has historically been high. For instance, solar photovoltaic panels and wind turbines require substantial upfront costs, mostly due to the intricacy of the technology. Over time, however, these costs have been decreasing. According to the International Renewable Energy Agency (IRENA), between 2010 and 2019, the cost of solar photovoltaic panels declined by 82%, and onshore wind turbine prices dropped by almost 40%.

Operational costs for renewable technologies are significantly lower than for fossil fuel-based systems. They generally require less maintenance and do not involve recurring fuel expenses. This means once the initial investment is recovered, renewable energy systems can be extremely cost-effective in the long run.

9.2. Payback Periods

The payback period is the time it takes to recover the initial investment through the savings offered by renewable technologies. Several factors influence this period, including the type of technology and location (which impacts resource availability), the local cost of electricity or heat, and any applicable government incentives.

For many residential solar photovoltaic systems, for example, the payback period is usually within a range of 5 to 10 years. For wind energy, the payback period can be anywhere from 6 to 15 years.

9.3. Government Incentives

Government policies and incentives play a significant role in encouraging investments in renewable energy. These incentives, designed to offset the initial costs, typically come in the form of tax credits, rebates, grants, or feed-in tariffs (payments to ordinary energy users for the renewable electricity they generate).

In the United States, for example, the Investment Tax Credit (ITC) allows for a deduction of up to 26% of the cost of installing a solar system from federal taxes. On the other hand, the U.K. government provides feed-in tariffs to encourage the use of renewable energy.

9.4. Economies of Scale and Market Conditions

Renewable energy investments benefit significantly from economies of scale, i.e., the cost advantage that arises with increased output of a product. As more of these systems are produced and installed worldwide, costs due to research, design, and manufacturing decrease, making these systems progressively more affordable.

Market conditions, including fluctuations in the price of fossil fuels and the evolving regulatory environment, also influence the cost-effectiveness of renewables. With the mounting pressure to mitigate climate change, regulations have been increasingly favoring renewable technologies.

9.5. Socio-Economic Implications

The shift to renewable energy can also have profound socio-economic implications, with the potential to generate substantial employment and foster economic development. According to IRENA, the renewable energy sector could employ up to 28 million people by 2050, up from approximately 11 million in 2020.

In conclusion, while the transition to renewables necessitates a substantial initial investment, the long-term returns outweigh these costs. Reduced operating costs, shorter payback periods facilitated by government incentives, and the socio-economic benefits arising from job creation and economic development all contribute to making the renewable energy sector a sound and profitable investment. With continuous technological advancements and economies of scale, renewables are expected to become even more cost-effective, further promoting the shift to a sustainable energy future.

Chapter 10. Policy and Green Technology: Regulations Impacting Advancement

In the world of green energy, policy plays a crucial role. It defines a nation's energy trajectory and influences the potency of technological advancements. Regulations serve as levers that can both accelerate and constrain the growth of green technology. This chapter unpacks the multifaceted impact of policy and regulations on the advancement of green technology – focusing on renewable energy standards, subsidies, carbon pricing, trade policies, and emerging trends in global environmental governance.

10.1. Renewable Energy Standards

Renewable Portfolio Standards (RPS) and Feed-in tariffs (FiTs) are significant policy instruments targeting to optimize renewable energy generation. RPS mandates utility companies to source a specific proportion of energy from renewable resources. These legislations ensure a steady demand for renewable power, thus encouraging technology providers to innovate and reduce costs. However, the challenge often lies in setting the right renewable energy targets that can balance social, economic, and technological feasibilities.

On the other hand, FiTs are policies through which the government guarantees to purchase renewable energy at predetermined prices for an extended period. As a result, investors and technology developers are encouraged to explore renewables as they are shielded from the risks of price volatility. On the downside, an improperly calculated FiT might place a financial burden on consumers or could even lead to an unsustainable "boom and bust" scenario in renewable energy projects. Hence, intelligent policy planning is needed to minimize any adverse outcomes.

10.2. Subsidies and Tax Incentives

Around the globe, subsidies and tax incentives have significantly advanced the deployment of green technology. Whether it's production tax credits for wind power in the U.S. or capital grant schemes for solar PV in Germany, these policies have encouraged investment in renewable energy and resulted in economies of scale.

However, the effectiveness of subsidies and tax incentives remains controversial. Critics argue that they distort the energy market, creating inefficiencies and inhibiting innovation. It is worth noting that fossil fuel industries too receive substantial subsidies - something that further complicates the green transition. Therefore, while subsidies have a role to play in overcoming barriers, their design and implementation should be carefully scrutinized to ensure long-term sustainability in the green tech space.

10.3. Carbon Pricing: A Market Approach

Carbon pricing, either through carbon taxes or cap-and-trade systems, is a market-based approach to internalize the environmental costs associated with fossil fuels. It essentially puts a financial cost on carbon pollution, thereby encouraging investments in cleaner, green technologies.

However, the effectiveness of carbon pricing largely depends on the specific design of the scheme and the baseline price of carbon. If set too low, carbon prices might not be enough to stimulate the shift towards green technology; if too high, they could cause economic dislocation. Thus, it's imperative to engage in diligent policy dialogue to underscore the significance and setting of carbon pricing.

10.4. Green Trade Policies

Trade policies also play a crucial role in the global green tech revolution. Tariffs and trade restrictions can have either positive or negative implications for green technology deployment. For instance, low-cost solar panels from China have dramatically reduced the price of solar energy worldwide, contributing significantly to its adoption. However, such a trade dynamic has also sparked debates around job losses in domestic manufacturing sectors.

Developing a cohesive international trade policy that both stimulates the global green tech industry and safeguards domestic interests remains a significant challenge for policy-makers. This complex interplay between global trade and local impact underlines a need for a balanced and sustainable green trade policy framework.

10.5. Emerging Trends in Global Environmental Governance

As the world grapples with the urgent need to transition to cleaner energy, the role of international environmental governance is becoming increasingly significant. Policymakers must constantly adapt to new technological advancements, and alongside, it is crucial to foster international collaboration.

The Paris Agreement, for instance, has brought about a sea change in our global approach towards renewable energy and green technology. Despite its non-binding nature, it has successfully driven nations to pledge substantial reductions in their carbon footprints and enhance their renewable energy initiatives.

While the progress in green technology looks promising, the final success of this massive global endeavor is contingent on the synergy between enlightened policy, effective regulations, and relentless technological advancements. At this juncture, robust policy making and sincere multilateral collaborations are not mere options; they are prerequisites for the brave new world of green technology we aspire to build. Policymaking and green technology must go hand in hand if we are to achieve a sustainable energy future.

Chapter 11. Tomorrow's Technologies: Innovations on the Horizon

As we stand on the brink of a technological revolution that promises to alter the energy landscape, emerging green technologies offer a glimpse of what a sustainable future could look like. From solar cells to wind turbines, the means of harnessing renewable resources are becoming increasingly efficient and affordable.

11.1. Solar Technologies

Solar energy remains one of the most abundant and untapped resources on the planet. The widespread implementation of solar technologies hinges on our ability to develop efficient, cost-effective solutions.

11.1.1. Photovoltaic Cells

There have been many advances in the field of photovoltaic cells, or PV cells. These devices, commonly recognized as solar panels, convert sunlight into electricity. The latest iterations employ enhanced materials such as perovskite and organic polymers, promising high conversion efficiency and flexible installation.

New tandem cell technology stacks multiple layers of photovoltaic materials to leverage a broader spectrum of sunlight, significantly boosting the overall energy conversion rate. However, durability and stability still pose concerns, and further research is required.

11.1.2. Concentrated Solar Power

While less familiar than PV cells, Concentrated Solar Power (CSP) technologies offer immense potential. Here, mirrors or lenses concentrate a large area of sunlight into a small beam, which is used to heat up a fluid to generate steam, driving a turbine that produces electricity.

Current innovations are moving towards 'super-critical' CSP plants, that use ultra-high temperatures to generate thermodynamic efficiencies equivalent to conventional power plants. These plants aim towards 24-hour operation by using molten salt to store heat, further increasing the promise that CSP holds for our renewable future.

11.2. Wind Technologies

Wind power, harnessed by turbines, is yet another powerful alternative to fossil fuels. Enhancements in turbine design and technology have stimulated its rapid growth.

11.2.1. Offshore Wind Farms

As we venture further off land, offshore wind farms take advantage of the steady, potent winds unimpeded by terrain. The introduction of floating turbine technology unlocks the potential for installations in deeper waters, broadening the geographical scope for deployment. Such innovations could significantly boost global wind capacity and present a solution for countries with limited onshore wind opportunities.

11.2.2. Vortex Bladeless Turbines

Emerging from the innovative shadows are vortex bladeless turbines - a radical departure from the conventional spinning blades. These structures vibrate in response to the wind, converting the mechanical energy into electricity via an alternator. The absence of moving parts reduces maintenance costs and mitigates hazards to wildlife, all while operating silently.

11.3. Beyond Wind and Solar

While solar and wind power dominate the dialogue around renewable energy, there are numerous other exciting advancements on the horizon.

11.3.1. Hydrokinetic Energy

Harnessing the kinetic energy of flowing water—rivers, tides, or artificially created channels—could serve as a reliable source of electricity. Innovative turbine designs and advanced construction materials can channel this energy, making hydrokinetic technology a viable and environmentally friendly alternative.

11.3.2. Bioenergy

Bioenergy or energy derived from organic materials has been used by humans for centuries. What's new is the development of advanced biofuels, produced from non-food crops, waste materials, and algae. These fuels have less of an impact on food prices and biodiversity than traditional biofuels and could serve as a greener substitute for fossil fuels in transportation.

11.3.3. Geothermal Energy

Enhanced Geothermal Systems (EGS) are designed to expand the potential of geothermal energy by accessing the Earth's heat beyond conventional reach. EGS artificially creates reservoirs in hot, dry rocks and circulates a heat-absorbing fluid. The heated fluid is used to generate electricity at the surface. This technology could expand the geothermal footprint worldwide.

While we traverse this unparalleled journey of energy transformation, the road ahead remains fraught with challenges and unknowns. Engineering virtuosity must go hand in hand with policy guidance and market strategies. The goal is clear—a sustainable energy future—and as these technologies mature, we inch steadily closer to realizing this vision. Through continued innovation, investment, and implementation, tomorrow's technologies can revolutionize our world and usher in a new era of green power.